AF261521

My Wonderful Life

An Adoption Story

Nicholas Battle

2020

My Wonderful Life: An Adoption Story
NinosCorner Productions LLC

First Printing: 2020

Illustrator: Tejal Misty

Website: www.NinosCorner.com

Email: Nino@NinosCorner.com

ISBN 978-1-7333570-6-7 (Hardcover)
ISBN 978-1-7333570-7-4 (Ebook)
ISBN 978-1-7333570-8-1 (Paperback)

Dedication

To the many adopted children in the world…
you are someone's dream come true.

Hello, my name is
Landon, and I
want to share my
story with you.

You see, I have two amazing parents. My Mommy is the sweetest person in the world. She gives me hugs and kisses every day. She also gives me my favorite snacks when my Daddy is not looking.

My Daddy is my super
hero. He throws the ball
and rides bikes with me.
I always feel safe when
my Daddy is around.

I am so blessed to have such an awesome Mommy and Daddy, but, for as amazing as my parents are, I am extremely blessed in many more ways than I can describe.

But, how can a kid like me be any
more blessed than I already am?
Well, let me tell you how.

My Mommy and Daddy tell me all the time that I am a special child. Not only do I have an amazing Mommy and an awesome Daddy, I also have birthparents.

You might be asking
yourself, "What are
birthparents?" Well,
let me explain.

My birthparents are the two parents who made me. They love me sooooo much, just like Mommy and Daddy.

When I was born, my birthparents
wanted the absolute best for me.
In order for me to have the
best, they allowed my Mommy and
Daddy to take care of me.

In order for my Mommy and Daddy
to take care of me, they had to
adopt me. I am soooo fortunate
to share my adoption story
with you!

Being adopted is no different
than not being adopted, except,
instead of 2 parents that love me,
I now have 4: my Mommy, my Daddy,
my Birth-Mother, and my
Birth-Father.

Although I do not see my birthparents all the time, my Mommy and Daddy always give them updates on how I am doing.

My birthparents even call me on my
birthdays to wish me a very happy
birthday. It's so kind and
thoughtful.

My Mommy and Daddy also share pictures
of my birth family so I will
always know my history.

My birthparents always see me excelling
and doing tremendous things.

Every time my birthparents see me doing so well, it reassures them that they made the absolute right decision for my well-being.

I know all adoption stories are not identical, and your story may not be exactly like mine. But our stories are common in a few ways.

As adopted children, we all have birthparents who love us so much that they made the unselfish decision to choose adoption as the best option for our future.

We also all have families that love us unconditionally and have given us the opportunity to live our best life possible.

Like my Mommy and Daddy said before,
I am a very special child...a
very special child loved by many.

Landon

You are the heartbeat of this family. The joy and happiness that you have brought to our lives is indescribable. When you came into our home, we realized that you were the missing piece to make our family whole, and we are forever grateful to your birthparents for making such an unselfish decision to choose adoption. Our hopes and dreams for you are infinite. You deserve all that the world can offer. Words cannot describe how much we love you.

Love,
Mommy and Daddy